Contents

How to use this book

There are hundreds of different plants and animals to spot in the woodlands of Britain and Europe. This book shows you some of them and helps you identify them.

Name and description of species

➡ **Stag beetle**

Largest British beetle. Only male has antlers. Larvae feed on tree stumps for three years or more. 25-27mm.

Average size

Identification

Each different kind of animal or plant is called a species. The descriptions next to each picture tell you what details to look for, where you are likely to find the species and how big it might be.

Picture of species (not drawn to scale)

Male and female

The males and females of some species can be different from each other. The symbols male ♂ and female ♀ show you which is which.

Male and female pheasant

♂

♀

4

Woodland Life

Edited by Sue Jacquemier and Sarah Khan

Consultant: Harry Pepper, from The Tree Advice Trust

Usborne Quicklinks

The Usborne Quicklinks Website is packed with thousands of links to all the best websites on the internet. The websites include information, video clips, sounds, games and animations that support and enhance the information in Usborne internet-linked books.

To visit the recommended websites for Spotter's Woodland Life, go to the Usborne Quicklinks Website at **www.usborne-quicklinks.com** and enter the keywords: **spotters woodlands**

Internet safety

When using the internet please follow the internet safety guidelines displayed on the Usborne Quicklinks Website. The recommended websites in Usborne Quicklinks are regularly reviewed and updated, but Usborne Publishing Ltd is not responsible for the content or availability of any website other than its own. We recommend that children are supervised while using the internet.

Usborne Publishing is not responsible and does not accept liability for the availability or content of any website other than its own, or for any exposure to harmful, offensive, or inaccurate material which may appear on the Web. Usborne Publishing will have no liability for any damage or loss caused by viruses that may be downloaded as a result of browsing the sites it recommends.

What lives where?

The animals and plants in this book can be found in the areas shown in dark green on this map. A few of the species described may be very rare where you live. They may be common in other European countries, though, so you might have a chance to spot them if you go abroad.

Scandinavia

The British Isles

Mainland Europe

Keeping a record

There's an empty circle next to each picture. Whenever you spot a species for the first time, you can put a tick in the circle.

Cep

Scorecard

At the end of the book is a scorecard. It gives an idea of how common each species is. The most common species score 5 points and the rarest types score 25. If you want, you can add up your score after a day out spotting in the woods.

Species (name)	Score	Date spotted
Robin	5	
Roe deer	15	14/03
Rowan	5	21/11
Saffron milk cap	10	

You can fill in the scorecard like this.

Measurements

The animals and plants in this book are not drawn to scale, but the descriptions next to the pictures tell you their size. Here you can see how they are measured.

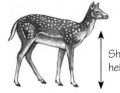

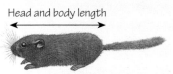

Head and body length

Hoofed mammals: shoulder height in metres or centimetres

Shoulder height

Small mammals: length of head and body, not including tail, in centimetres

Length

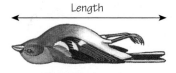

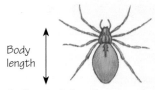

Body length

Birds: length of bird from beak to tip of tail, in centimetres

Spiders: body length, not including legs, in millimetres

Wingspan

Body length

Butterflies and moths: wingspan, in millimetres

Other insects: body length, not including antennae, in millimetres

Width of cap

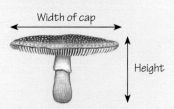

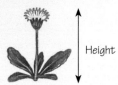

Height

Fungi: width of cap or height from ground level, in centimetres

Height

Flowers, trees and ferns: height from ground level, in centimetres or metres

How to watch wildlife

Being prepared

When you're going out into the woods, it's best to wear layers of waterproof, light clothing in dull colours, to help you blend in with the scenery. Take this book to help you identify the plants and animals you spot. You might also want to take a notebook in which you can jot down your findings.

Keeping quiet

A good way to explore a wood is to walk slowly and quietly through it, looking around as you go. When you find a convenient, sheltered spot, sit there quietly for a while and be on the look-out for animals passing by.

Respecting nature

When visiting woods and forests, always remember to follow this code:

- Never light fires
- Keep to the paths, and close gates behind you
- Keep dogs under control
- Don't damage hedges, fences, walls or signs
- Look, don't touch: leave plants, animals and nests alone
- Take your litter home with you

It's best to be quiet when you're out spotting, because shy animals, like this young fox, might run away if they hear you coming.

Broadleaved woods

Trees in broadleaved woods have wide, flat leaves.
Between autumn and spring, they shed their old leaves
and begin to grow new ones. This allows sunlight through
the branches onto the floor below. Plants and animals
thrive in these sunny conditions.

   In most broadleaved woods there are more of
one type of tree than another, often depending on
conditions such as the type of soil.

Leaf shapes

Leaves from broadleaved trees can either be in a single
piece or made up of smaller parts called leaflets.

On common alder
trees, the leaves
are in one piece.

Common ash leaves
have several leaflets
on one stalk.

Horse chestnut
leaflets are arranged
in a hand shape.

Leaves in autumn

If you visit a broadleaved wood during autumn, you might
notice that the leaves on the trees are no longer green. As
winter approaches, the dominant green colouring in leaves
breaks down and other colours are revealed.

Maple

Sycamore

Rowan

Beech

Horse chestnut

English oak

8

Broadleaved woodland life

In spring, a broadleaved wood is busy with life. Flowers carpet the floor and hang from branches; animals, just woken from hibernation, search for their first good meal in months; and birds fly to and fro, collecting material for their nests.

You might see any of these plants or animals in a broadleaved wood.

Coniferous woods

Coniferous woods are dark and dense, as they are made up of trees that don't drop all their leaves in autumn like broadleaved trees do, but shed them little by little steadily throughout the year. Most conifers have long, skinny leaves called needles. Not many plants can grow on coniferous woodland floors because of a lack of light and a permanent layer of needles on the ground.

Needles

Almost all conifer leaves are either slim needles or stubby scales. They grow in different arrangements, shapes and sizes.

The needles on Scots pine trees grow in pairs.

Swiss stone pine needles grow in bunches of five.

Like most cypresses, a Lawson cypress has scale-like leaves.

Cones

Conifer trees bear cones instead of fruit. Most cones are covered in scales, under which seeds grow.

Atlas cedar trees grow large, barrel-shaped upright cones.

Long Norway spruce cones hang down from branches.

The cones that grow on yew trees look like berries.

Coniferous woodland life

Coniferous woods are thick and shady, and provide shelter for shy animals such as deer and pine martens. Mosses, ferns and fungi grow well over the ground and up the sides of trees.

Here are some of the animals and plants you might see in a coniferous wood.

Trees

↑ English oak

Broad-crowned tree with many large branches growing upwards from the same point. Look for short-stalked leaves with ear-like lobes at the base.

23m

Tall acorns on long stalks

Lobe

Stalk

Acorn cup

Cluster of "keys" (fruits)

↑ Common ash

Pale grey bark and compound leaves of 9-13 leaflets, appearing late, after bunches of purplish flowers. Clusters of seeds stay on the tree into winter.

25m

Mitre-shaped bud

Flowers

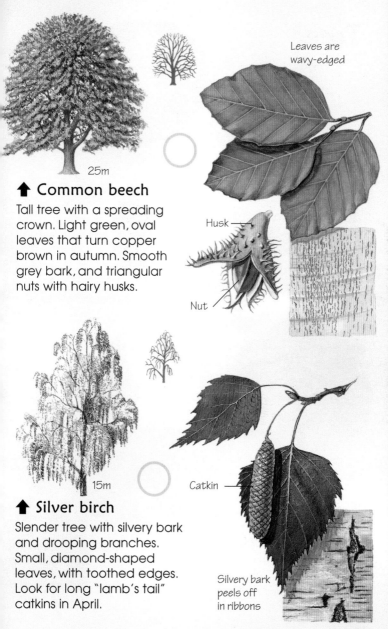

Leaves are
wavy-edged

↑ Common beech

Tall tree with a spreading
crown. Light green, oval
leaves that turn copper
brown in autumn. Smooth
grey bark, and triangular
nuts with hairy husks.

25m

Husk

Nut

↑ Silver birch

Slender tree with silvery bark
and drooping branches.
Small, diamond-shaped
leaves, with toothed edges.
Look for long "lamb's tail"
catkins in April.

15m

Catkin

Silvery bark
peels off
in ribbons

13

Trees

Leaf has notched tip

12m

↑ Common alder

Rounded leaves fall in late autumn. Reddish catkins and small, brown, woody cones. Sticky young twigs and leaves. Often found near water.

Cones stay on all winter

Leaves have toothed edges

20m

↑ Sycamore

Large spreading tree, with dark green leathery leaves with toothed edges and five lobes. Look for paired, right-angled, winged fruits spiralling away from the tree on autumn winds. Smooth brown bark, becoming scaly.

Fruits twist as they fall

⬆ Sweet chestnut

Clusters of edible brown
chestnuts in prickly cases.
Long, narrow leaves with
saw-toothed edges. Bark
sometimes spiral-furrowed.

25m

Female
flowers

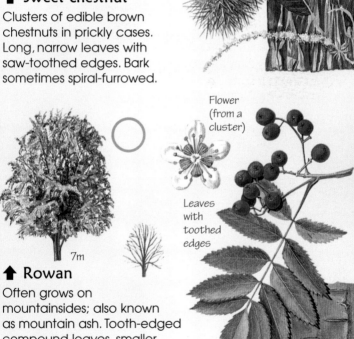

Flower
(from a
cluster)

Leaves
with
toothed
edges

Leaves turn red
in the autumn

⬆ Rowan

Often grows on
mountainsides; also known
as mountain ash. Tooth-edged
compound leaves, smaller
than other ashes. Clusters of
creamy-white flowers in May,
and red berries in August.

7m

Trees

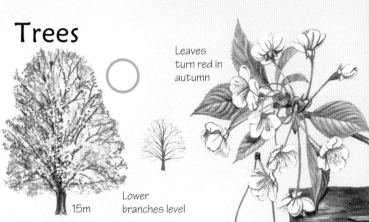

Leaves turn red in autumn

Lower branches level

15m

↑ Wild cherry

White blossom in April and red, edible (though sour) cherries. Large, pointed, oval leaves with toothed edges. Reddish-brown bark peels in ribbons.

Red cherries contain single stones

Horizontal marks on shiny bark

10m

↑ Holly

Small tree with shiny, dark, evergreen leaves with thorny prickles. Small, white flowers in April and May. Look for round, red berries for rest of the year. Smooth grey-green bark.

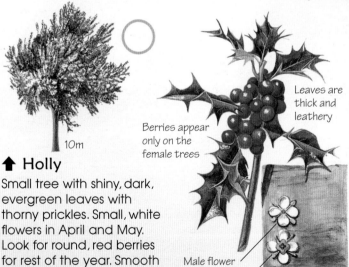

Berries appear only on the female trees

Leaves are thick and leathery

Male flower
Female flower

Catkin "pussy willow"

Underside of leaf

↑ Goat willow

Broad, rounded, rough, grey-green leaves. Look for silvery-grey upright catkins, known as "pussy willow", in late winter. Small bushy tree. Common in damp areas.

7m

The crown shape varies

Leaf stalks are long and flattened

↑ Aspen

Rounded leaves with wavy edges, deep green on top, paler beneath. White downy catkins. Grey bark with large irregular markings. Often found growing in thickets.

20m

17

Trees

10m

↑ Hornbeam

Sharply toothed, oval
leaves. In autumn, clusters
of three-pronged, leaf-like
wings hold nuts. Smooth,
grey bark is fluted or rippled.

Cluster of
green winged
fruits

Tree in flower

8m

↑ Hawthorn

Shiny, deeply lobed,
dark green leaves and
thorny twigs. Clusters
of small, white flowers
in May, and dark red
berries. Rounded crown.

Berries
called
haws

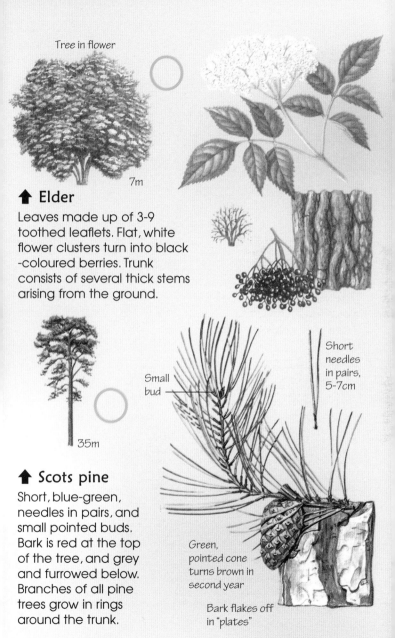

Tree in flower

7m

↑ Elder

Leaves made up of 3-9 toothed leaflets. Flat, white flower clusters turn into black-coloured berries. Trunk consists of several thick stems arising from the ground.

35m

Small bud

Short needles in pairs, 5-7cm

↑ Scots pine

Short, blue-green, needles in pairs, and small pointed buds. Bark is red at the top of the tree, and grey and furrowed below. Branches of all pine trees grow in rings around the trunk.

Green, pointed cone turns brown in second year

Bark flakes off in "plates"

19

Trees

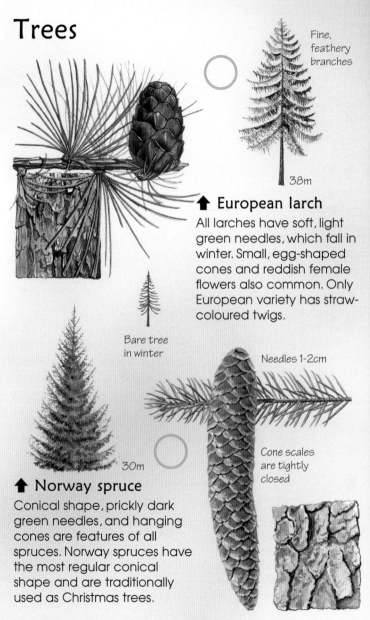

Fine, feathery branches

38m

↑ European larch

All larches have soft, light green needles, which fall in winter. Small, egg-shaped cones and reddish female flowers also common. Only European variety has straw-coloured twigs.

Bare tree in winter

Needles 1-2cm

Cone scales are tightly closed

30m

↑ Norway spruce

Conical shape, prickly dark green needles, and hanging cones are features of all spruces. Norway spruces have the most regular conical shape and are traditionally used as Christmas trees.

Large, upright cones

Bracts showing

Rare in Britain, but common in central Europe

Very tall, narrow tree

40m

The twigs are smooth and the needles have notched tips

↑ European silver fir

Flat single needles, green above and silvery below. Look for flat, round scars left on twigs when needles drop. All firs have cylindrical cones that stick up from the branches.

Wide, spreading branches

15m

↑ Yew

Often seen in churchyards as a wide, spreading tree or as a hedge. Poisonous needles and fruit. Needles are dark green above and yellowish below. Look for orange-brown flaking bark.

Birds

◀ Nightjar
Rarely seen in daylight.
Listen for churring call
at night when it hunts
insects. Nests in
clearings. 27cm.

➡ Sparrowhawk
Broad-winged hawk.
Hunts small birds
along hedges and
woodland edges.
Never hovers.
Female 38cm;
male 30cm.

♂

*Notice the
pale wing
patches*

◀ Buzzard
Large bird of prey with
broad wings. Nests in woods,
often returning year after
year. Rarer in southern and
eastern England. 54cm.

➡ Tawny owl
Calls with familiar "hoot".
Hunts at night in woods.
Eats small mammals or
birds. 38cm.

➡ Great spotted woodpecker

Size of a blackbird. Found in woods all over Britain. Listen for the sound of it drumming on trees with its beak in spring. 23cm.

Large white patches on wings

Yellow-green rump

♂

⬅ Green woodpecker

Pigeon-sized. Often feeds on ground. Found in open woods. Quite common in England and Wales. Rare in Scotland. Listen for its laugh-like call. 32cm.

➡ Lesser spotted woodpecker

Sparrow-sized. Lacks white wing patches of great spotted woodpecker. Male has red crown. Open woodland. Not in Scotland. 14cm.

Stripy back

♂

Woodpeckers do not live in Ireland. They all have bouncing flight.

23

Birds

Female's cap is reddish-brown

♂ ♀

← Blackcap

Common summer visitor to woods. Always moving from perch to perch as it sings. 14cm.

→ Willow warbler

Summer migrant. Most common British warbler. Its song, which comes down the scale, is the best way of telling it from the chiffchaff. 11cm.

Pale legs

← Chiffchaff

Summer migrant, often arriving in March. A few spend the winter here. Sing repetitive "chiff-chaff" song from cover in woods. 11cm.

Dark legs

→ Wood warbler

Summer migrant to open woods. Sings from a branch, repeating a note faster and faster until it becomes a trill. 13cm.

Yellow breast, white underparts

➡ Marsh tit

A bird of deciduous woods, like the willow tit (not illustrated). Rarely visits gardens. 11cm.

No pale patch on wings

Northern and eastern Europe

Britain and western Europe

⬅ Long-tailed tit

Look for groups of these tiny birds on the edges of woods. Loud, trilling song. 14cm.

➡ Garden warbler

Summer visitor. Sings from dense cover and is hard to see. Breeds in woods. Song can be confused with blackcap's. 14cm.

Brown above, paler below

⬅ Coal tit

Likes conifer woods, but often seen in deciduous trees. Look for large white patch on back of head. 11cm.

25

Birds

← Pied flycatcher

Catches insects in air.
Also feeds on the ground.
Summer migrant to old
woodland. 13cm.

➜ Redstart

A summer migrant to
open, particularly oak,
woods. Constantly flicks
its tail. 14cm.

White stripe
over eye

Firecrest

Goldcrest

← Firecrest
← Goldcrest

Smallest European birds.
Goldcrests are found in
woods, especially of pine,
all over Britain. Firecrests
are much rarer. 9cm.

➜ Robin

Common woodland bird.
Sings in winter and spring.
"Tic-tic" is its call of alarm. Male
and female look alike. 14cm.

➡ Chaffinch

Prefers coniferous woods but can be seen in deciduous woods, too. Often flocks with other finches in winter. 15cm.

Crossbills are sparrow-sized, with large heads and bills

⬅ Crossbill

Nests in pine woods. A slightly different species nests in Scotland. Eats pine cone seeds. 16cm.

➡ Siskin

A small finch which nests in conifers. It sometimes visits gardens in winter to feed on peanuts. 11cm.

Lesser redpoll

Common redpoll

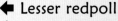

⬅ Lesser redpoll
⬅ Common redpoll

The lesser redpoll is common in birch woods and forestry plantations in Britain. The common redpoll lives in northern Europe. 12cm.

27

Birds

← Woodcock

Secretive bird of damp woods.
Rests in dense cover during the
day. Watch out for its bat-like display
flight over woods at dusk in early summer.
Rapid, zig-zag flight pattern. 34cm.

→ Woodpigeon

Largest of the
pigeons. Breeds
and spends winter
in woodlands. White
neck and wing patches
clearly visible in flight.
Forms large flocks.
Cooing call. 41cm.

White on
wings

← Nuthatch

Deciduous woods in
England and Wales. Very
short tail. Climbs up, down
and around trees in a
series of short hops using
its powerful toes. Nests in
holes in trees, which it may
plaster with mud. 14cm.

➡ Pheasant

Lives on the edges of woodlands. Often reared as game. Male has a loud, screeching call. Roosts in trees, nests on ground. Male 87cm; female 58cm.

♂

Males can vary in colour and often have a white neck ring

♀

⬅ Treecreeper

Usually seen in woods climbing up tree trunks and flying down again to search for food. Often joins flocks of other small birds in winter. Listen for high-pitched call. 13cm.

➡ Jay

Shy woodland bird. Rarely moves from cover. Listen for harsh screeching call. Look for white rump in flight. Buries acorns in autumn which it digs up to eat when other food supplies are low in winter. 32cm.

Mammals

➡ Red deer

Lives in herds on woodland edges. Young have spotted coat. Eats grass, heather, fruit and tree bark. Sometimes raids crops. 1.5m.

Summer coat

Tips of antlers stretch out like fingers

⬅ Fallow deer

Young are heavily spotted. Shelters in woods. Eats grass, acorns buds, bark, berries and fungi. 1m.

Summer coat

➡ Roe deer

Grey-brown in winter. Lives near water on its own or in small groups in conifer plantations. Eats leaves, berries and herbs. 70cm.

⬅ Red fox

Common in woodlands. Usually comes out only at night. Preys on small mammals, birds and even young deer. 65cm.

 Fore foot Hind foot

➡ Badger

Active at night. Lives in family groups in networks of tunnels called setts, mainly under woods. Eats worms, roots, small animals and plants. 80cm.

Fore foot   Hind foot

⬅ Polecat

Rare in Britain. Can be seen in wooded areas, often near houses. Eats small mammals, eggs and frogs. Lives on its own and comes out at night. 40cm.

Hind foot   Fore foot

➡ Pine marten

Shy mammal of mountain woods. Good climber. Comes out at night. Eats small mammals, birds, insects and berries. 50cm.

Hind foot   Fore foot

Fore foot Hind foot

⬅ Bank vole

Widespread in deciduous woods and hedgerows. Active by day. Climbs well and makes its burrows in banks. Eats buds, berries, insects and bark. 10cm.

Short, blunt nose

Mammals

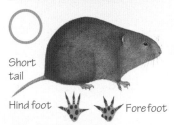

Short tail

Hind foot   Fore foot

← Short-tailed vole / field vole

Active by day. Makes tunnels below open ground. Not found in Ireland. Eats grass, roots and bark. 11cm.

➡ Wood mouse

Active at night. Good climber and jumper. Digs burrows. Eats buds, berries, seeds and nuts. 9cm.

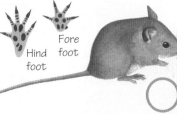

Fore foot

Hind foot

Hind foot   Fore foot

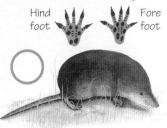

← Common shrew

Solitary and aggressive towards other shrews. Climbs and swims. Common in woods. Not found in Ireland. Eats insects and worms. 7cm.

➡ Common dormouse

Nocturnal and solitary. Lives in shrubs and bushes in woods. Eats seeds, insects, nuts and berries. 8cm.

Fore foot

Hind foot

Hind foot   Fore foot

← Pygmy shrew

UK's smallest mammal. Habits similar to common shrew. Found in young conifer woods. 5cm.

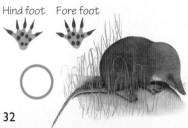

Ear tufts

Fore foot   Hind foot

← Red squirrel

Rare, shy mammal, seen mostly in coniferous woods. Eats seeds of cones, buds, berries, bark and nuts. 23cm.

→ Grey squirrel

Much bolder than red squirrel. Coat may have patches of brown in summer. 27cm.

Fore foot

Hind foot

← Rabbit

Digs network of burrows called a warren. Lives in colonies. Eats plants. 40cm.

Hind foot   Fore foot

Long ears with black tips

Fore foot

Hind foot

→ Brown hare

Silent and solitary. Feeds in open areas. Rests in woodland during the day. Eats plants. 58cm.

Legs are longer than a rabbit's

Fungi

➡ Saffron milk cap

Common under conifers in autumn. Develops green stains as it ages. When touched, drips a milky liquid which turns red. 7cm.

Green stains

Red liquid

Caps turns red-brown as the fungi age

⬅ Wood blewit

Blue-violet and waxy. Grows well on leaf litter from October to December. 8cm.

➡ Deceiver

Often grows in groups under light tree covering. Very common in woods in summer and autumn. Red-brown with pinkish tinge. 4cm.

Widely spaced gills with white powder on edges

Gills run halfway down stem

⬅ Paxil

Brown cap with woolly, incurved edge. Summer and autumn. Very common in woods, especially birch. 9cm.

➡ Chanterelle

Often grows in groups on mossy woodland floors. Look for it in summer and autumn. Bright yellow all over. Firm in texture with mild, apricot fragrance. 7cm.

Gills run all the way down stem

⬅ Wood mushroom

Fairly common growing under conifers in summer and autumn. Look for smooth, reddish-brown scales on cap. Strong almond scent. 7cm.

Broad ring on stem

➡ Cep

Stem has white net of veins. Common in autumn under broadleaved trees, especially beech. 13cm.

Grows in clumps from stumps and trunks

⬅ Honey fungus

Can be seen in clusters from late summer to autumn. Spreads dark bootlace-like growths into tree roots to feed. Often kills its host. 8cm.

35

Fungi

➤ Funnel cap

Fairly common in woods from summer to autumn. Look for slightly silky cap and hairs at base of stem. 6cm.

Funnel-shaped cap

Bright red cap

◀ Sickener

Brittle white gills. Common under birch and pine in late summer and autumn. Can cause sickness if eaten. 7cm.

➤ Red milk cap

Very common under pines in summer and autumn. Bitter, milky liquid oozes from gills when touched. 6cm.

Shiny cap

◀ Death cap

Deadly if eaten. Grows mainly under beech and oak from August to September. Cap is streaked brownish green or bright yellow. 9cm.

Bulge at base of stem, covered by a white sheath

➡ Fly agaric

Contains several different poisons. Tall, with a bulbous base and ring around the stem. Common under birches in autumn. 11cm.

White warts on scarlet cap

Ring

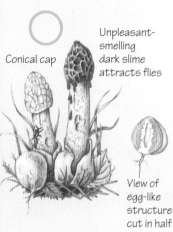

Conical cap

Unpleasant-smelling dark slime attracts flies

View of egg-like structure cut in half

⬅ Stinkhorn

Grows up from white egg-like structures in leaf-mould. Usually appears overnight after rain. On emerging, the cap is covered with dark slime. Height from ground level 15cm.

➡ Tall veil cap

Fairly common in autumn, especially under beech. Poisonous. Covered by a web-like veil when young. 7cm.

Brown cap with violet tints

Rusty colour under cap

Stem is red with network of veins

⬅ Bitter boletus

Light greyish-brown cap. Grows in mixed woodlands in late summer and autumn. 12cm.

37

Wild flowers

◄ Lesser celandine

A small, creeping plant with glossy, heart-shaped leaves. Shiny yellow flowers. Look in damp, shady woods and waysides from March to May. 7cm.

Flowers grow in rings around the stem

➤ Yellow archangel

Also called weasel-snout. Look for the red-brown markings on the yellow petals. Opposite pairs of leaves. Common in woods in May and June. 40cm.

◄ Primrose

Well-known spring flower, with hairy stems and rosette of large leaves. Often grows in patches. Flowers in woods from December to May. 15cm.

◀ Wood woundwort

Spikes of dark red and white flowers in whorls. Smells strongly. The leaves were once used to dress wounds. Look in woods between June and August. 40cm.

➡ Foxglove

Erect plant with tall spike of tube-shaped flowers, drooping on one side of the stem. Large, oval leaves. Flowers from June to September in open woods. Up to 150cm.

Sepals

Bud

◀ Common dog violet

Creeping plant with rosettes of heart-shaped leaves. Look for the pointed sepals and short spur on the flower. Found in woods between April and June. 10cm.

Wild flowers

➡ Lesser periwinkle

Creeps along the ground with long runners, making leafy carpets. Shiny, oval leaves. Look in woods and hedges between February and May. Stems grow up to 15cm.

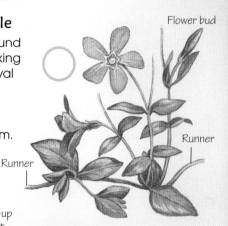

Flower bud

Runner

Runner

Close-up of fruit

⬅ Bluebell

Also called wild hyacinth. Narrow, shiny leaves and clusters of nodding blue flowers. Forms thick carpets in woods in April and May. 30cm.

➡ Bugle

Creeping plant with erect flower spikes. Glossy leaves in opposite pairs. Stem is square and hairy on two sides. Leaves and stem are purplish. Forms carpets in damp woods in May and June. 20cm.

Close-up of bugle-shaped flower

◀ Wood sorrel

A creeping, woodland plant with slender stems and rounded leaves. White flowers with purplish veins. Flowers in April and May in woods and hedges. 10cm.

➡ Wild strawberry

Small plant with long, arching runners and oval, toothed leaves in threes. Sweet, red fruits, covered with seeds. Look in woods and scrubland between April and July.

The large sepals look like petals

◀ Wood anemone

Also called Granny's nightcap. Forms carpets in woods from March to June. The flowers have pink-streaked sepals. 15cm.

41

Wild flowers

➡ Dog's mercury

Downy plant with opposite, toothed leaves. Strong-smelling. Male flowers grow on separate plants from female flowers. Found in patches in woodlands from February to April. 15-20cm.

Plant with only male flowers

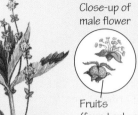

Close-up of male flower

Fruits (found only on female plant)

Close-up of single flower

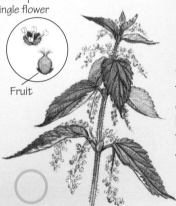

Fruit

⬅ Nettle

The toothed leaves are covered with stinging hairs. Dangling green-brown flowers appear between June and August. Used to make beer and tea. Common. Up to 100cm.

➡ Cuckoo pint / lords and ladies

Flowers hidden inside green hood. Leaves sometimes have dark spots. Grows in shady woods from April to May. Up to 45cm.

Hood

Fruit appears in autumn and is poisonous

42

Other plots

➡ Bracken

Like all ferns, has leaf-like
structures called fronds.
Bracken fronds are broad,
light green and feathery,
becoming rust coloured
in autumn. Dies away in
winter. 1-2m.

⬅ Cushion moss

Grows well in damp
conditions on ground and
bark. Attaches itself with
little root-like structures. Tiny
leaves spiral around stem.

➡ Leafy lichen

Common in old broadleaved
woods, especially on trees with
ridged bark, such as oak and
ash. Grows well in clean air and
sensitive to air pollution.

⬅ Yorkshire fog

Grass with soft, grey-green,
hairy leaves. Flowers can
be white, pale green, pink
or purple. 20-100cm.

Butterflies

➡ Speckled wood

Often settles in sunny spots in woods and forests. Attracted to bramble flowers. Caterpillar eats grasses. 47-50mm.

♀

Orange-brown European form of speckled wood

♂

⬇ Comma

Look for its ragged wing edges and the c-shaped marking on the underside of its wings. Seen in woodland clearings. 56-58mm.

⬇ White admiral

Flies around tree tops, but may come down to drink from mud or to visit flowers such as bramble. Caterpillar feeds on honeysuckle. 44-58mm.

♂

♂

➡ Purple emperor

One of Britain's largest
butterflies. Drinks from
woodland puddles.
Males fly around
treetops. Caterpillar
eats goat willow
leaves. 76-84mm.

♀

Purple sheen on
wings is visible in
bright sunshine

♂

♀

Thistle

⬅ High brown fritillary

Attracted to thistle
flowers. Rests on
high branches in woods on
dull days. Caterpillar feeds
on violet leaves. 60-68mm.

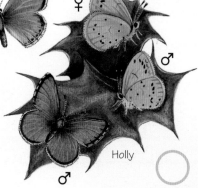

♀

♀

♂

➡ Holly blue

Visits holly and ivy
plants. Feeds from
flowers and on unripe
berries. Sometimes drinks
by edges of streams.
Appears slightly silvery in
flight. 33-35mm.

Holly

♂

Moths

← Leopard moth

Females can sometimes be seen resting on tree trunks. Larvae are rarely seen as they feed inside tree trunks and branches. Female 65mm; male 40mm.

➡ Goat moth

Widespread, but well camouflaged and rarely seen. Larva smells like goats and eats wood of ash and willow. Spends three or four years in a tree trunk. 70-85mm.

Peach blossom pattern

← Peach blossom

Common in woodland areas. Its name comes from the peach blossom pattern on its wings. Larva feeds on bramble. 35mm.

➡ Merveille-du-jour

Lives in oak woodlands. Forewings match oak tree bark, making moth difficult for enemies to see. Larva eats oak leaves. 45mm.

← Peppered moth

Usually spotted, but some forms are black all over. Twig-like larva feeds on leaves of trees and rose bushes. 50-60mm.

→ Green oak tortrix

Larva common in midsummer. Feeds inside a rolled-up oak leaf and suspends itself from a silk thread if disturbed. 20mm.

← Bordered white

Males are dark brown with yellowish white blotches. Larva feeds on conifers and can damage trees. 30-35mm.

♀

→ Pine hawk moth

Fairly common in conifer woods. Look for it resting on tree trunks. Larva feeds on conifer needles. 70-90mm.

Beetles

➡ Nut weevil

Female uses her long rostrum to pierce a young hazelnut, into which she lays a single egg. Larva grows inside the nut, eating the kernel. 10mm.

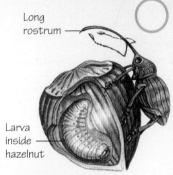

Long rostrum

Larva inside hazelnut

⬅ Pine weevil

Look on conifers such as pine and spruce. Adults eat young shoots. Eggs are laid in older tree stumps. Larvae feed on bark and wood. 10-15mm.

➡ Leaf-rolling weevil

Adults roll up birch and alder leaves and lay eggs inside. On hatching, the larvae eat the leaves. 3-5mm.

1

2

3

Weevil cuts leaf in two places.

It rolls leaf into a tube.

Eggs are laid inside.

48

Antlers

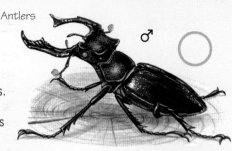

♂

➡ Stag beetle

Largest British beetle.
Only male has antlers.
Larvae feed on tree
stumps for three years
or more. 25-27mm.

⬅ Ant beetle

Small, fast-moving beetle
found on elms and conifers.
Larvae live under loose bark.
Both larvae and adults eat
larvae of bark beetles.
7-10mm.

➡ Longhorn beetle

Can be seen on flowers
along woodland paths.
Makes a buzzing sound as
it flies. Larvae feed in old
tree stumps. 15-20mm.

Tunnels made
by larvae

⬅ Oak
bark beetle

Found on oak trees.
Female lays eggs along
the sides of a tunnel
it makes in the tree. On
hatching, larvae burrow
at right angles to their
mother's tunnel. 3-4mm.

Beetles

← Violet ground beetle

Nocturnal. Body is black with a violet sheen. Rests under logs and stones during the day. Adult and larva eat other insects and worms. 30-35mm.

→ Eyed ladybird

Britain's largest ladybird. Found near or on fir trees. Both adults and larvae hunt for aphids. 8-9mm.

Fir

Larva

♀

♂

← Glow-worm

Found in open woods. Wingless female attracts male with its brightly glowing tail. Males, larvae and eggs also glow faintly. Male 15mm; female 20mm.

Bugs and crickets

➡ Common shield bug

Look on oak, alder and fruit
trees. Adults use their
mouthparts to pierce
and suck fluids
from larvae. 15mm.

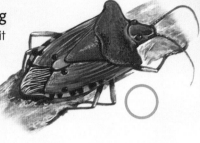

*Gall
shaped like
pineapple*

⬅ Spruce aphid

Lays eggs on spruce and
larch shoots. As larvae
feed, they cause the shoots
to swell up, forming galls.
1-2mm.

➡ Scale insect

Larvae live inside small,
scaly shells on leaves,
stems and fruits of various
trees. Both the larvae and
the wingless females feed
under the shells. 2-3mm.

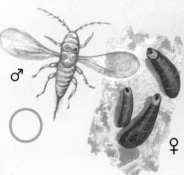

♂

♀

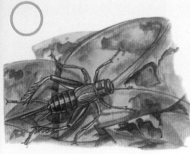

⬅ Wood cricket

Found in piles of dead
leaves in ditches and
banks. Male has quiet,
churring song.
Flightless. 8-9mm.

Wasps and sawflies

➡ Giant wood wasp / horntail

Female lays eggs in sickly or felled conifers. Larvae feed on wood for up to three years. 25-32mm.

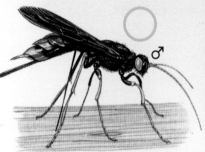

♂

♀

⬅ Ichneumon wasp

Female pierces pine trees with her ovipositor and lays an egg on a horntail larva or in its burrow inside the tree. 22-30mm.

➡ Hornet

Nests in hollow trees, banks or roofs. Preys on soft-bodied insects which it feeds to its larvae. Also feeds from flowers in woods. 22-30mm.

Dog rose

⬅ Birch sawfly

Name "sawfly" comes from female's saw-like ovipositor. Larva feeds on birch leaves in late summer. It makes a large oval cocoon and the adult emerges the next spring. 20-23mm.

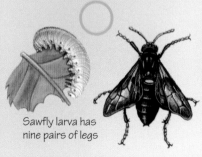

Sawfly larva has nine pairs of legs

Ants, centipedes and millipedes

➡ Wood ant

Makes large conical nest from twigs and leaves in pine woods. Useful to foresters as it feeds on leaf-eating larvae. Cannot sting, but sprays formic acid at intruders. 5-11mm.

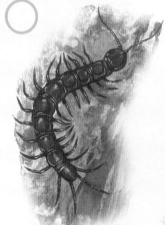

⬅ Centipede

Found under leaf litter and stones, and in the bark of old trees and soil. Feeds on small insects, larvae and worms. 20-30mm.

➡ Millipede

Usually has about 100 pairs of legs. Found in damp spots under bark and leaf litter. 30mm.

Spiders

➡ Hunting spider

Lives in a funnel in the centre of a large, greyish web. May also be seen hunting in open woodland. Female carries its eggs in a sac. 15mm.

Egg sac

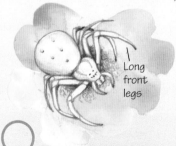

Short legs and large eyes

⬅ Zebra spider

Has no web, but stalks its prey, then leaps on it. Crawls with a jerky movement. Look on tree trunks and in sunny spots. 5-7mm.

➡ Garden spider / cross spider

Look for white cross-shaped group of spots on abdomen. Hangs head down in the centre of its web. 6-18mm.

Long front legs

⬅ Crab spider

Lurks on flowers waiting for insects. Can change colour and can also scuttle sideways like a crab. 5-10mm.

Winter buds

In winter, many trees have no leaves, but you can often identify them by their winter buds. These contain the beginnings of next year's shoots, leaves and flowers. You can tell one tree from another by looking at the shape of the twigs, the colour and shape of the buds, and by whether the buds are sticky, scaly or hairy.

↓ Common ash

Large, black opposite buds on smooth, silver-grey twigs.

↓ Common beech

Long, pointed, copper-brown buds sticking out from brown twigs.

↓ Wild cherry

Fat, shiny, red-brown buds grouped at the tips of light brown twigs.

↓ Sweet chestnut

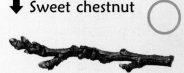

Rounded, reddish-brown buds on knobbly, greenish-brown twigs.

↓ Sycamore

Green, opposite buds, with dark edged scales on light brown twigs.

↓ Turkey oak

Clusters of small, brown, whiskered buds, growing alternately on brown twigs.

Reading rings

Tree trunks are made up of ring-shaped layers of wood. Each year, a trunk thickens by growing a new layer. If you come across a tree stump in a wood, you'll see a pattern of rings all the way across it. By counting these annual rings, you can tell how many years old the tree was when it was cut down.

You can also find out a lot more about a tree's life story by looking at its rings.

The wider the ring, the more the tree grew that year. Trees grow well when they get plenty of water, light and air, in hot, rainy seasons, or when the other trees around them are cut down. They don't grow well in seasons of floods or droughts, or when they are in crowded conditions.

This dent shows that the tree was damaged a long time ago.

A year with lots of growth

A year with little growth

Useful words

These pages explain some words you might come across when reading about flowers, trees, birds and insects. Words that are written in *italic text* are defined separately.

ambush – a surprise attack from a hidden position

antenna (plural: **antennae**) – one of a pair of feelers on an insect's head used for feeling and smelling

antlers – bony extensions that grow from the head of members of the deer family

bark – a tough outer layer that protects a tree's insides

bract – a leaf-like part of a cone supporting the seed

broadleaf – a tree that has wide, flat *leaves*. Most broadleaved trees are *deciduous*

bud – an undeveloped *shoot*, *leaf* or *flower*

bug – an insect with sucking mouthparts, and forewings that are thickened and leathery at the base

burrow – a hole in the ground made by an animal for shelter

cap – (1) the top part of a bird's head (2) the top part of a *fungus*

catkin – an often sausage-shaped cluster of tiny *flowers*, all of the same sex, growing on one *stalk*

clearing – an area of land with little or no trees in the middle of a wooded area

cocoon – a skin or case in which some insect *larvae* rest as they turn into adults

colony – a group of animals of the same *species* living together

compound leaf – a type of *leaf* made up of smaller *leaflets*

cones – the *fruits* of *conifers*

conifer – a tree with needle-like or scaly *leaves*, which bears *cones* with their *seeds* inside. Most are *evergreen*.

corolla – all a flower's *petals*

cover – anywhere that animals hide themselves, for example hedges, bushes or thick grass

creeping plant – a plant that grows low along the ground

crown – (1) the collective name given to a tree's branches, twigs and leaves (2) the top part of a bird's head

deciduous – a tree that loses its *leaves* over a few weeks, usually in autumn

evergreen – a tree that loses its *leaves* throughout the year, so it is always green

fern – a flowerless plant that has *fronds* instead of *leaves*, and *spores* instead of *seeds*

flower – the part of a plant where new *seeds* are made

fore foot – the front foot of a four-legged animal

forewings – the front pair of wings on an insect

frond – the *leaf*-like part of a *fern*

fruits – the parts of a plant that hold its *seeds*

fungi (singular: **fungus**) – simple, plant-like living things that typically feed off dead or living animals and plants

gall – a swelling of plant tissue caused by insects feeding

gills – ribs or plates on the underside of a *fungus cap*

heath – windswept, open area of treeless land

herd – a group of *mammals* that live together

hind foot – the back foot of a four-legged animal

hoof – the hard, horny casing covering the toes or lower part of the foot of certain *mammals*

host – a plant or animal that is attacked by a *parasite*

hover – when a bird or insect stays in one place in the air by flapping its wings very fast

kernel – the inner and usually edible part of a *seed*, grain, nut or fruit stone

larva (plural: **larvae**) – the young stage of an insect which is very different from the adult insect

leaf – flat, thin outgrowth of a plant's *stem* that is usually green. Leaves make food for the plant.

leaflets – *leaf*-like sections that make up a *compound leaf*

leaf litter – mixture of fallen and dead plant material on the ground, made up of *leaves*, *bark*, *stems* and branches

leaf-mould – rotting *leaves*

lobe – a section of a *leaf* or *leaflet*

mammal – a warm-blooded animal that has hair and feeds its young on milk

migrant – an animal that breeds in one area, then moves to another for the winter, returning again the following spring

nocturnal – active at night

ovipositor – a female insect's egg-laying organ

parasite – a living thing that feeds off another plant or animal without killing it

pasture – grassland used to provide food for farm animals

petal – a segment of the *corolla*, usually brightly coloured

roots – parts of a plant that grow into the ground, absorbing water and goodness from the soil and anchoring the plant

rosette – a circle of *leaves* growing from a single point

rostrum – the long, tube-like stabbing mouthpart of *bugs* and weevils

rump – the area of a bird's body above its tail

runner – a *stem* that grows along the ground

scales – (1) the tough, woody parts of a *cone* (2) a *bud's* outer layers

scrubland – an area of land covered with low shrubs, grasses, and herbs

seed – part of a flowering plant that may grow into a new plant

sepals – *leaf* or *petal*-like growths which protect the flower *bud* and support the *flower* once it opens

sheath – a protective layer

shoot – a young *stem* or twig bearing *leaves*

solitary – living alone

species – a group of plants or animals that all look alike, behave in the same way and can breed together

spore – part of a *fern* and *fungus* that may grow into a new plant

spur – a tube formed by the *petals* of some *flowers*

stalk – a slender *stem* that supports a *leaf* and attaches it to a larger stem of a plant

stem – the part of a plant that supports the *leaves* and *flowers*, and carries water and food around the plant

stump – the lower end of a tree remaining in the ground after most of the trunk has been removed

thicket – an area filled with plants, bushes and small trees growing close together

trill – a quick burst of very short notes, which all run together

toothed – jagged

trunk – the main woody *stem* of the tree that holds it upright

undergrowth – small trees, bushes and plants growing beneath taller trees in a wood or forest

Scorecard

When you start spotting, you'll soon find that some plants and animals are rarer than others. To give you a rough idea of how likely you are to see them, all the flowers, trees, birds, mammals and insects in the book are listed here with a score next to each one.

Species	Score	Date spotted	Species	Score	Date spotted
Ant beetle	15		Common alder	5	
Aspen	15		Common ash	5	
Badger	15		Common beech	5	
Bank vole	5		Common dog violet	10	
Birch sawfly	10		Common dormouse	20	
Bitter boletus	15		Common redpoll	15	
Blackcap	15		Common shield bug	10	
Bluebell	10		Common shrew	10	
Bordered white moth	10		Crab spider	10	
Bracken	5		Crossbill	15	
Brown hare	5		Cuckoo pint	10	
Bugle	10		Cushion moss	5	
Buzzard	15		Death cap	15	
Centipede	5		Deceiver	5	
Cep	10		Dog's mercury	10	
Chaffinch	5		Elder	5	
Chanterelle	10		English oak	5	
Chiffchaff	10		European larch	5	
Coal tit	10		European silver fir	10	
Comma	15		Eyed ladybird	15	

Species	Score	Date spotted	Species	Score	Date spotted
Fallow deer	10		Leaf-rolling weevil	10	
Firecrest	20		Leafy lichen	5	
Fly agaric	10		Leopard moth	15	
Foxglove	15		Lesser celandine	5	
Funnel cap	15		Lesser periwinkle	15	
Garden spider	5		Lesser redpoll	10	
Garden warbler	15		Lesser spotted woodpecker	20	
Giant wood wasp	15		Longhorn beetle	15	
Glow-worm	15		Long-tailed tit	10	
Goat moth	15		Marsh tit	15	
Goat willow	5		Merveille-du-jour	15	
Goldcrest	10		Millipede	10	
Greater spotted woodpecker	10		Nettle	5	
Green tortrix moth	5		Nightjar	15	
Green woodpecker	15		Norway spruce	5	
Grey squirrel	5		Nuthatch	15	
Hawthorn	5		Nut weevil	5	
High brown fritillary	5		Oak bark beetle	10	
Honey fungus	5		Paxil	5	
Holly	5		Peach blossom	10	
Holly blue	10		Peppered moth	10	
Hornbeam	10		Pheasant	5	
Hornet	10		Pied flycatcher	15	
Hunting spider	10		Pine hawk moth	20	
Ichneumon wasp	15		Pine marten	20	
Jay	10		Pine weevil	15	

61

Species	Score	Date spotted	Species	Score	Date spotted
Polecat	20		Sweet chestnut	5	
Primrose	10		Sycamore	5	
Purple emperor	25		Tall veil cap	15	
Pygmy shrew	15		Tawny owl	15	
Rabbit	5		Treecreeper	10	
Red deer	15		Violet ground beetle	5	
Red fox	10		White admiral	15	
Red milk cap	10		Wild cherry	5	
Red squirrel	15		Wild strawberry	15	
Redstart	15		Willow warbler	10	
Robin	5		Wood anemone	10	
Roe deer	15		Wood ant	10	
Rowan	5		Wood blewit	10	
Saffron milk cap	10		Wood cricket	15	
Scale insect	10		Woodcock	15	
Scots pine	5		Wood mouse	10	
Short-tailed vole	5		Wood mushroom	15	
Sickener	10		Woodpigeon	5	
Silver birch	15		Wood sorrel	5	
Siskin	15		Wood warbler	15	
Sparrowhawk	15		Wood woundwort	20	
Speckled wood	5		Yellow archangel	10	
Spruce aphid	10		Yew	20	
Stag beetle	15		Yorkshire fog	5	
Stinkhorn	10		Zebra spider	5	

Index

Designed by Stephanie Jones and Joanne Kirkby
Digital manipulation by Mike Olley and Keith Furnival

Illustrated by John Barber, Amanda Barlow, Joyce Bee, Isabel Bowring,
Trevor Boyer, Hilary Burn, Christine Darter, John Francis, William Giles, Victoria
Goaman, Victoria Gordon, Tim Hayward, Christine Howes, Ian Jackson, Andy
Martin, Malcom McGregor, Annabel Milne, Barbera Nicholson, Chris Shields,
Annabel Spencely, Peter Stebbing, Phil Weare and others

PHOTO CREDITS: Cover © NHPA / LAURIE CAMPBELL; 1 © Scott Tilley / Alamy;
2-3 © Bob Barnes / Alamy; 7 © Ed Maynard / Alamy

This edition first published in 2009 by Usborne Publishing Ltd,
83-85 Saffron Hill, London EC1N 8RT, England. www.usborne.com.
Copyright © 2009, 1985, 1979 Usborne Publishing Ltd. The name Usborne
and the devices ♀ ♟ are Trade Marks of Usborne Publishing Ltd.